Usborne
Can we really HELP the Polar Bears?

YES you can.

The Children
Helpful Road
WARM LAND

Katie Daynes

illustrated by Róisín Hahessy

designed by Helen Lee

Right, I've checked the map. Everyone ready?

Let's go!

ARCTIC

There's much less ice than last year.

From the Arctic

Dear Children,
WE NEED YOUR HELP!
We're heading South to explain why.
Please tell your friends.
See you soon.
Love from,

The Polar Bears

P.S. This is serious!

The Children
Helpful Road
WARM LAND

NORTH

SOUTH

Wow – real polar bears coming to visit US!
We'd better get ready to welcome them!

Thank you so much for having us.
We wouldn't normally bother you...

...but we've been
having a tough time.

Why? What's wrong?

Cookie?

It's a long story...

We like stories!

You see, we're used to life in the freezing cold, hanging out on huge chunks of floating ice.

Brrrrr
Sounds chilly!

It's not chilly for us in our thick fur coats.

The frozen Arctic is our home and the ice is our hunting ground.

When a tasty seal pokes its head above water...

...we POUNCE!

But now our home is MELTING.

And without the ice to hunt from,
we're going to go VERY hungry.

Another cookie?

Yes please.

But WHY is the ice melting?

Well, it all started many years ago...

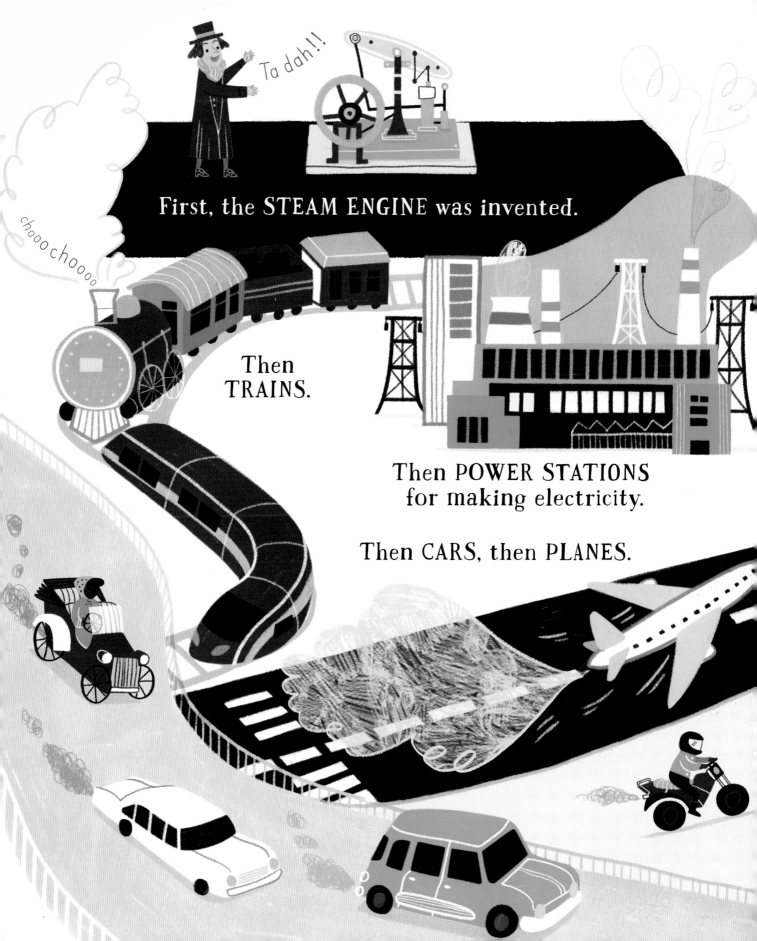

First, the STEAM ENGINE was invented.

Then TRAINS.

Then POWER STATIONS for making electricity.

Then CARS, then PLANES.

All these inventions work
by burning stuff called
FOSSIL FUELS.

Fossils?

Like the ones you
find on the beach?

Yes, a little like them.

I found a fossil
with my Gran
last summer.

Gran it's
MASSIVE!

FUELS are things you burn to make heat or power.
And FOSSIL fuels are fuels made from
ancient plants and animals.

They've been squashed underground
for millions of years

and have turned into

thick, black OIL

an invisible GAS

and dry, dusty COAL.

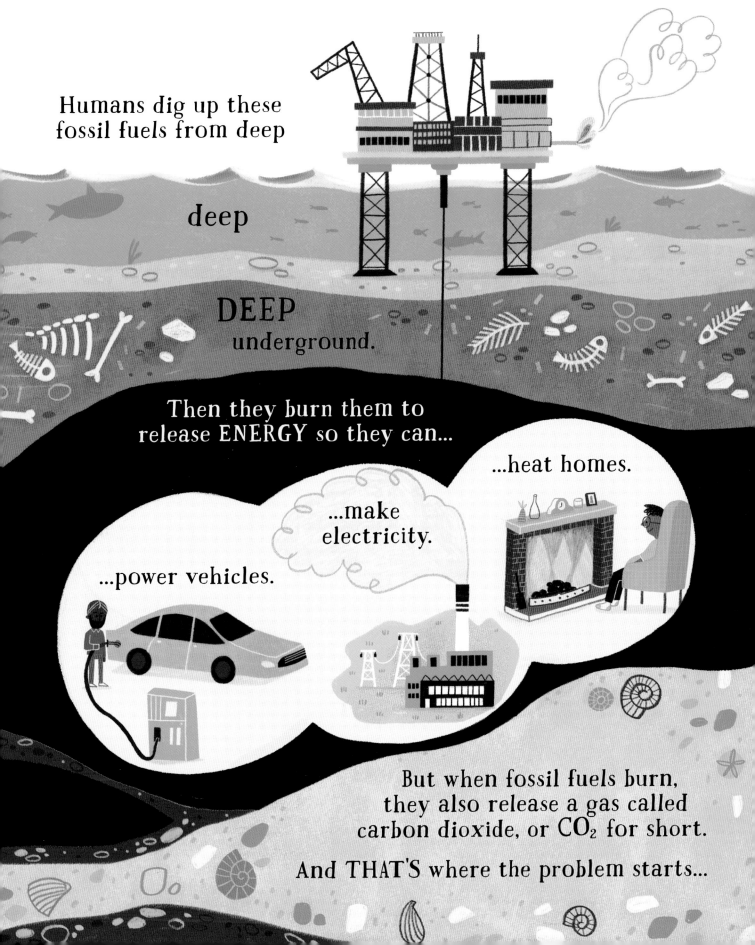

You see, CO_2 is a **GREENHOUSE** gas.

What's a GREENHOUSE gas?!

It's a gas that traps in heat.
It works like glass in a greenhouse.

Rays from
the sun heat up
the ground...

I know what a
greenhouse is — my
Gran has one!

...and the
greenhouse traps in
some of that heat.

It helps my plants to grow.

Greenhouses keep plants
warm, and greenhouse gases
keep our planet warm.

We need SOME greenhouse
gases in the air around us.

BRRRRRR

Without them, the sun's heat
would escape back into space.

And even the polar
bears and penguins
would freeze!

BRRRRR

But adding MORE greenhouse gases is BAD NEWS.

They trap in MORE HEAT
and make the planet WARM UP.

So **THAT'S** why your ice is melting! And why you can't hunt for seals.

Um, why don't you eat something else instead?

They don't have cookies in the Arctic.

This isn't just about feeding the polar bears. A warmer planet will affect **ALL** of us!

MEOW!

Eeeeeep!

But if it gets warmer
we can play outside more!

We can go to the
beach and swim in the sea...

...even in winter!

I'm afraid warmer temperatures
AREN'T good news for everyone.

Already, they're causing
all kinds of problems...

In some places, **wild storms** are making too much wind and rain.

In other places, the sun is too HOT, the rain won't fall and forests are BURNING.

People and animals sometimes struggle to get the food they need.

Meanwhile, our seas are **rising**.

The seawater expands as it gets warmer and creeps up the land.

Baaaa!

Melted ice runs off the mountains and fills up the sea **EVEN MORE.**

Homes and farms are getting flooded.

HELP!

We need a PLAN.

Let's make a list of the problems, then think up some solutions.

GREENHOUSE GASES

PROBLEMS

Making electricity

Powering vehicles

Heating homes

SOLUTIONS

I've forgotten – why is making electricity such a problem?

Because over half of the world's electricity comes from burning fossil fuels, making

LOTS of CO_2.

Let's try to use LESS electricity then.

We can SWITCH THINGS OFF when we're not using them.

Hey, who unplugged the house?

Sorry Ma'am.

We need to stop burning coal.

But there are also BETTER ways of making electricity in the first place.

You can make electricity from the **whizzing** of the wind...

the **shining** of the sun...

Wind turbine

Solar panel

...and the **whooshing** of water.

THEY don't create nasty fumes or greenhouse gases. So they're called CLEAN ENERGY SOURCES.

Let's use them then!

There's a house on my street with solar panels.

And wind turbines on the hill near me!

SOLUTIONS

CLEAN ENERGY

What about VEHICLES?
How do THEY make greenhouse gases?

By burning FUEL inside their engines, which gives off CO_2 and other nasty fumes.

Pooo-eey

My Uncle's got an ELECTRIC car.
Is that any better?

YES! Because it doesn't burn fuel and make nasty gases.

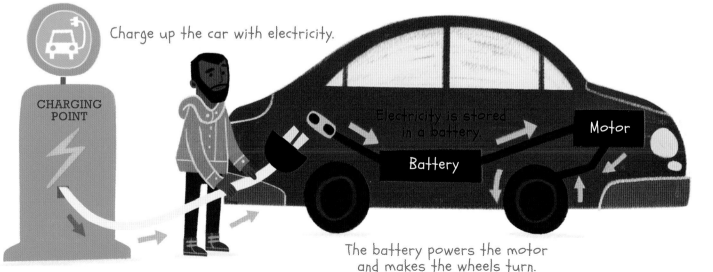

Charge up the car with electricity.

CHARGING POINT

Electricity is stored in a battery.

Motor

Battery

The battery powers the motor and makes the wheels turn.

Electric cars don't puff out nasty fumes.

Let's make ALL vehicles electric!

And let's charge them up with electricity from CLEAN ENERGY SOURCES.

I'm going to invent a car that runs on WATER.

I love it!

We're going to use our own legs
and arms to get around.

Muscle power is a very
clean source of energy.

But it would take HOURS
to walk to my Gran's.

**You could get a lift
with your cousins...**

One car is better than two!

...or you could go by train.
Trains make MUCH less CO_2 per passenger than cars.

What about flying?

Not good, I'm afraid. One plane gives off the same amount of CO_2...

...as 200 fossil fuel cars making the same journey.

And some plane journeys can be VERY LONG.

So why don't we make ELECTRIC planes?

Inventors are trying to...

We need a HUGE battery to store enough electricity for take-off.

Um, where do the passengers go?!

Battery

It won't budge!

...but until we can make better batteries, electric planes won't take us very far.

Let's try to FLY LESS then, while we solve the plane problem.

My Auntie can do her business meetings online.

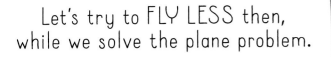

People can have adventures closer to home.

There's a campsite near me.

Great! Those solutions can go on the plan.

Powering vehicles

Share cars

Use muscle power

Trains NOT planes

Camping near home

Houses with extra padding keep in more heat.

The padding goes INSIDE the walls, so it doesn't get soggy.

It's called insulation.

Insulation

Ooh toasty.

And you can heat your homes with CLEAN ENERGY.

Why don't we just move to a warmer country?

If the world keeps getting warmer, we might not NEED heating!

Ah, but people in hot countries make greenhouse gases too, trying to COOL their buildings.

Hot
Cold

Air conditioning units use electricity to take heat out of the air.

Air conditioning unit

Why not close shutters instead, to block out the heat?

Or grow trees for shade?

And paint the walls white so the hot sun bounces off them.

Those are brilliant ways to keep cool without warming up the world.

Yes, food can make lots of greenhouse gas.

Especially if it's flown in from faraway countries...

REPAIR

buy less stuff

RE-USE

RECYCLE

...or grown under heat lamps.

And if you throw food away, then that's bad too.

Oops, we made too much.

Why?

Because growing and preparing food makes CO_2 whether you eat it or not!

FOOD PROCESSING

LANDFILL SITE

And burying food makes another greenhouse gas called METHANE.

Gosh. I'd better finish what's on my plate.

Or you could cook up
your leftovers the next day.

My Gran puts her food
waste in a compost bin.

It turns into a rich soil
for my garden.

COMPOST

We love your Gran!

Mr. Polar Bear, is it true that
cows and sheep BURP OUT
greenhouse gas?

BURP

No way!

Yes they do.
That's methane too.

So it's not just OUR
fault that the planet
is getting warmer.

You should talk to the cows as well.

Excuse me, Mrs. Cow. Can you stop burping please?

Tee hee

The thing is, most cows are only here because humans want them for their meat or milk.

I love a chocolate milkshake.

I make a yummy beef stew.

So... should we stop eating meat?

Eating LESS beef and lamb would help. And you'd be helping the forests too.

The FORESTS? What have THEY got to do with meat?

They're being CUT DOWN to make space to grow and feed farm animals.

You see, you need **10 times** more land to farm BEEF...

...than you do to farm PLANTS.

Meat burger

Veggie burger

I like trees...

...but I think I like meat more.

It's not as if we need so many trees in the world.

YES WE DO!

We need LOTS of them.
They're not just homes to amazing animals...

...they also **CLEAN THE AIR** for us!

They spend all day sucking up the CO_2 around them.

Then they store the C bit (carbon)...

...and let out the O_2 (which is oxygen, the gas we all need to breathe).

If you destroy a tree, the carbon turns into CO_2 again...

...but if you let it grow, it can suck up even more CO_2.

In that case, we must PROTECT our FORESTS.

And PLANT MORE TREES.

And do everything else on our plan!

Let's start right NOW!

We can check things off as we do them.

□ Plant more trees.

Eat less meat.

□ Buy less stuff.

Remember to REDUCE   RE-USE   RECYCLE

□ Eat food that's in season.
(Grown locally or sent by ship)

□ Use electric vehicles...

COLD DAYS

□ Wear a sweater.

HOT DAYS

Make some shade.

But we can only REALLY help the polar bears if EVERYONE joins in!

Let's tell our parents and teachers.

Emergency meeting for all parents and teachers

It's a problem we all need to solve.

We should write to big businesses too. They can make A LOT of CO_2.

Here's the company address.

PROBLEMS

Making electricity

Powering vehicles

Heating and cooling buildings

Factories

Food

Farming

FOSSIL FUELS

...ASES

SOLUTIONS

- use CLEAN ENERGY
- switch things OFF
- use LESS energy

- walk or cycle
- go by train NOT plane
- car share
- use ELECTRIC vehicles
  (that run on CLEAN ENERGY)

- turn down the heat
  (and wear more clothes)
- add better insulation
- make more shade in
  hot countries

- make less stuff
- only use CLEAN ENERGY
- REDUCE, RE-USE, RECYCLE

- don't fly food around
  the world
- eat food that's in season
- don't waste food
- eat less meat

- protect our forests
- PLANT MORE TREES

LEAVE THEM
   IN THE GROUND

And talk to our politicians – they make the rules.

This is excellent. I'll tell the government.

GREENHOUSE GASES
PROBLEMS   SOLUTIONS

Let's send copies of our plan to the leaders of EVERY country and big business IN THE WORLD!

There are nearly 200 countries.

Brazil

Indonesia

YES! YES! YES!

Poland

Scotland

Spain

We CAN
help the polar bears!

Tweeeet!

And you'll be
helping the rest
of the planet too.

YES!

THANK YOU!

Yippee!

Hooray!

Brilliant!

We'll deliver these on our way.

Thanks so much for your help. Goodbye.

What next?

The problems the polar bears describe in this book are REAL and affect us ALL. The GOOD NEWS is that things are already changing...

In 2015, countries around the world agreed to work TOGETHER to stop the planet from warming up too much.

It's called the Paris Agreement, because it happened in Paris.

Sim Yes Oui Ja Yes 예 Yes 是 Ja

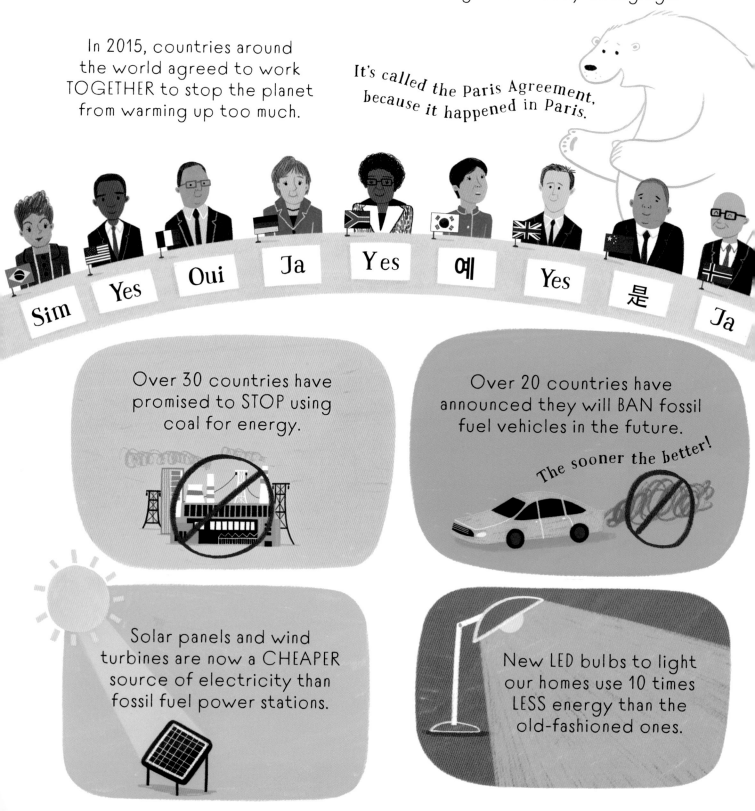

Over 30 countries have promised to STOP using coal for energy.

Over 20 countries have announced they will BAN fossil fuel vehicles in the future.

The sooner the better!

Solar panels and wind turbines are now a CHEAPER source of electricity than fossil fuel power stations.

New LED bulbs to light our homes use 10 times LESS energy than the old-fashioned ones.

There's still LOTS MORE TO DO and we'll all need to play our part to make a cleaner, greener future.

I'm going to be an INVENTOR and make a machine that sucks CO_2 out of the air.

I'm going to be a FOREST MANAGER and plant a billion native trees.

no. 3354

I'm going to be a WILDLIFE EXPERT and learn more about polar bears.

I'm going to set up a BUSINESS making water-powered cars.

I'm going to be an ARCHITECT and design houses that run on clean energy.

I'm going to be a TEACHER and teach others how to look after our planet.

WORK WITH NATURE

I'm going to be a POLITICIAN and make laws to stop air pollution.

Glossary

Here are some of the important words in
this book and what they mean.

air conditioning unit – an electric device used
to take heat out of rooms and cool them down

Arctic – the area around the North pole,
at the northern-most point of planet Earth

battery – a container for storing electricity

carbon dioxide – the greenhouse gas
people make when they burn fossil fuels

clean energy – energy made without
giving off nasty gases

CO₂ – short for carbon dioxide

compost – a rich kind of soil made
from food and garden waste

electricity – a way of getting energy
from one place to another. Lots of things
we use today need electricity to work.

fossil fuels – coal, oil and natural gas

greenhouse gas – a gas which traps in heat
when it's added to the air

insulation – a layer of padding to keep out the cold

methane – a greenhouse gas made when things rot underground or by cows and sheep burping

oxygen – the gas we all need to breathe in to live

power station – a factory that makes electricity

solar panel – a flat surface that can turn the sun's energy into electricty

steam engine – an invention that uses the power of steam to make things move

wind turbine – a tall pole with spinning blades that makes electricity from the wind

Usborne Quicklinks

Visit usborne.com/Quicklinks for links to websites where you can meet some real polar bears and find activities and videos about how we can help them.

Please follow the internet safety guidelines at Usborne Quicklinks. Children should be supervised online.

Edited by Jane Chisholm
Climate change expert: Dr. Steve Smith

Additional inspiration from Zoe Wray,
Mary Cartwright and the polar bears

First published in 2021 by Usborne Publishing Ltd., Usborne House, 83-85 Saffron Hill, London, EC1N 8RT. usborne.com